Dedicated to the memory
of my mom
Sallie Mae Keller

Moving My
Mountains
A Journey to Peace from Codependency

By Glenn C. Keller

Tribute
Publishing
2016

Copyright © 2016
Tribute Publishing
Frisco, Texas

Tribute
Publishing

Moving My Mountains
A Journey to Peace from Codependency

First Edition August 2016

All Worldwide Rights Reserved
ISBN: 978-0-9906001-1-4

All Rights Reserved. No part of this book may be reproduced, stored in a retrieval system, or transmitted, in any form, or by any means, electronic, mechanical, recorded, photocopied, or otherwise, without the prior written permission of the copyright owner, except by a reviewer who may quote brief passages in a review.

Printed in the United States of America

In God We Trust

Contents

A Tribute to Our Mother i

Chapter 1 – My Name is Glenn 1
   Poem – Mother's Day 7

Chapter 2 – When Did It Start? 9
   Poem – The Day I Got Tired 30
   Poem – Trying Desperately to Cope 31
   Poem – Knowing His Divine Will 35

Chapter 3 – How Did I Find Out? 39
   Poem - Mom I'm going to be All Right 51

Chapter 4 – Moving Towards Peace 53
   Poem – Thinking of You 63

Chapter 5 – The Way Out 65

About the Author 81

Sallie Mae Keller

A Tribute to Our Mother

In the beginning God created the heavens and the earth…
It was Sallie Mae Keller who on August 13, 1928
Rosella Hutchinson was allowed to give birth…
Who knew that 32 years later mom would give birth to me…
Then 2 years later add my beautiful sister to the family tree…
Let our testimony be that mom was always there…
Let it be that mom always loved us and would always care…
These stomachs never knew hunger not one single day…
These feet were never bare, no how, no way…
Mom would do without before she would allow us to…
That's not strange, that's just what good mothers do…
One thing mom would never be was our playmate or our friend…
Mom knew it was a parent upon which we needed to depend…
When we wouldn't get it through our heads that we were supposed to do right…
It was through our other end that mom made us see the light…
Mom loved all and was loved by many…
Mom would give her last and not turn her back on any…
Mom we celebrate your life because that is what we do…
When you love someone as much as we love you.

…Your children,
Glenn & Carol

Chapter 1

About Glenn

Chapter 1 – About Glenn

Life began for me in New Orleans, Louisiana, where I was born in 1960 to Preston and Sallie Keller. I seem to see my life growing up in a couple of ways: I see it as I lived it growing up and I see it looking back on it. Seeing my life as a child growing up it could not have been better. However, looking back on my life I find myself asking, "Where were the hugs, kisses, and positive affirmations?" My sister and I seemed to have everything we could have ever wanted. We wore nice clothes to school, we were never hungry, and I remember us having all the latest toys, which back then was a bicycle, some skates, and some toy soldiers. My earliest memories are when I was around three years old going to preschool. You would have thought that I was being tortured when it was time to get on the school bus because I didn't want to leave my momma. Mom was very protective so we didn't go over to other children's houses to play. The yard was as far as we were allowed to go and that was under strict supervision, meaning the watchful eye of mom.

I was about five when things changed drastically, and although I say drastically now, at the time I was actually too young to be phased by it. Mom was up early one morning sewing as she often did, when Carol (my sister) and I got up. Carol would never eat breakfast without dad and she told mom she was hungry. Mom told us to go wake up dad so that we could have breakfast. We ran into the bedroom where mom and dad slept, jumped on the bed, and did what we could to wake up dad, but he didn't move. Well, we were kids and didn't think anything of it, especially when Carol ran back to where mom had been sewing and said, "Momma,

Chapter 1 – About Glenn

daddy is playing like he's dead." Mom got up and came into the room where dad had been sleeping and the next thing I heard was a scream like I had never heard before, nor have I heard since. Mom became a single parent that day.

Mom moved to New Orleans with a 9th grade education and married our dad. To this day, I still don't know a better business woman than mom was. She bought two other homes besides the one we were born in, and at one point had purchased at least a dozen pieces of rental property. Mom was my hero; she was amazing and there was no one in the world like her. I remember working so hard, doing everything I could to make her proud. I now think I got everything I needed growing up, except what I may have needed most.

I mentioned having a vivid memory back to the age of three, and I do remember most things. Things like catching the bus for preschool, everything about finding my dad after he had passed away in his sleep, and how a couple of years later, on a Sunday, someone came to the church we attended to get us because our house was on fire. I actually could go on and on about the things I remember from my childhood. You know, it's not the things about my childhood I remember, it's actually the things that I don't remember that have caused me heartache, pain, and tears. No matter how hard I try to think about it I can't ever, and I mean ever, remember hearing the words, "Come here and give mommy a big hug" or "Mommy loves my baby." I didn't hear, "I'm so proud of you." Those are the memories I desperately wish I had. I was a child; I didn't know I was going to need to

Chapter 1 – About Glenn

hear those things to make me whole, to make me healthy. I had no way of knowing what I was missing. It was a very long time before I realized I was even supposed to hear those things and how important they are to the development of a child.

There is one thing I remember hearing as a young boy that I've never forgotten, nor do I think I will ever forget. As best I can remember, this one negative remark was the only thing along that line, and I'm glad there was nothing else like it. It would happen at family functions like reunions and other family gatherings. It would happen while surrounded by aunts, uncles, cousins, and friends of the family. I would run up to mom, probably wondering if I would hear some of the things that I never did. Instead, what I heard was, "Do you wash your face? There's nobody in our family that black." I was hurt, embarrassed, and I felt ugly and unloved.

Let me catch everyone before anyone rushes to judgement on my mom. Okay, she didn't say the things I wanted to hear and as it turned out, needed to hear. Knowing what I know now, positive affirmations and 'I love you' may not have been the things that were said to her when she was growing up as a little girl. In defense of my mommy, and I'll defend her until the day I die, what she didn't say, she more than showed. I feel like she showed it every morning when she got up for those 32 years, put on that white uniform dress and white shoes that I would see her polishing every night, and went to work in those hot, school cafeterias. I saw it in the nice clothes my sister and I wore that we never

Chapter 1 – About Glenn

had to pay for. I saw it in the meals we ate that didn't cost us a dime. I saw it in a roof that was always over our heads without ever having to pay a mortgage payment or rent.

Let me share this experience with you that may tell you everything you need to know about why I loved my mom so much. It was after I had begun driving trucks for a living that I would always find my way back to my mom's house for Mother's Day. The Monday morning after one particular Mother's Day, mom left early to run some errands. Well, when it was time for me to leave, I turned to lock her door and when I turned back around (to walk down what was maybe four or five steps) I fell, tried to catch myself with one hand, and shattered my wrist. What was supposed to be an overnight visit turned into a seven-month stay. There I was, back in my old room. One day my wrist was hurting really bad. I had been given a prescription for Percocet for the pain. On this day, I took my medication and had no choice but to lie down. That stuff was powerful. I was resting so mom thought it would be a good time to go to the store. Mom's house was on the corner, so when she pulled from in front of the house and drove through the intersection, she saw smoke coming from what looked like the back of her house and the place where I lie sleeping. When mom backed up and opened the front door, the house was filled with smoke. A fire had started in the back room next to where I was sleeping. With the house filled with smoke and the room next to me ablaze, my mom, my mommy, my momma, made her way through the smoke to the back room where I laid asleep and oblivious to the fire that was raging in the next room. I've always been bigger than my small mom, but that day she was Wonder Woman because it was her and her alone that got me all the way though that smoke-filled house and out the front door to safety. Need I say, had it not been for my mom who gave me life one day and turned around and saved my life on another day, there would have been no Glenn Keller, no Making Difference Ministries, no Sallie and Son Unlimited, and no Empowerment Express.

So if there were some things she didn't say when I was a child, or some things she should not have said, she was so forgiven. I can't even tell you how much she was forgiven. It didn't prevent me from wishing I had the benefit of hearing those words growing up. A lot of my childhood was spent trying to make her proud, trying to get those affirmations, but to no avail. During the time before my mom passed away, she told me how much she appreciated me trying to take care of her while having to work and run a business and be on the road all the time. She expressed to me that she felt like if it wasn't for me, she would have been in a nursing home. That was something she never wanted and I never wanted it for her. I was constantly thinking of options in case I had to get off the road to take care of my mom.

If there is such a thing as speaking from the grave, then my mom did it in a big way. I never heard the words from her mouth, but when mom transitioned, I heard them from the mouths of those she had told it to. My mom would always tell her friends how proud she was of everything I had ever done or accomplished. I was told, at times, she would

Chapter 1 – About Glenn

just go on and on about me and what I was doing. It may not have been directly from my mom's mouth, but for me it was the same as if it had. She spoke to me from the grave and I found a way to speak back to her with poetry.

Mother's Day

Every day seemed like Mother's Day as far as I knew

When I think of all you would say on top of all the things you would do

I must have been five when Carol and I found dad passed while asleep in bed

It was the day you not only became a single mom but also became the head

You never missed a beat as far as I could tell

You were Wonder Woman and in all you did mom you excelled

Left with two babies to raise you always did your best

No matter what life threw your way you always passed the test

It could not have been easy in that hot school kitchen those 32 long years

I'm sure there were times your heart was heavy and eyes filled with tears

Chapter 1 – About Glenn

You were the best thing that could have happened to Carol and I

That's what made it so hard when it came time to say goodbye

I can never forget how you gave me life one day and then saved it on another

Who else would have entered that burning and smoke-filled house to save me except a loving mother?

These poems are my way of talking to you while others listen in

After all, I'm the proud son of Sallie Mae Keller and my name is Glenn.

Chapter 2

When Did It Start?

Chapter 2 – When Did It Start?

What came first, the chicken or the egg? What came first, the low self-esteem, poor self-worth, or codependent behavior? My life wasn't off to a good start to having any real self-worth at all. As much as I talked about early childhood memories back to the age of three, there is a space of time that I don't remember how old I was, but I remember clearly what happened to me. I had a relative who would come in town during the summer for a week, and before the summer had ended I would visit him and his parents. I'm not sure how many summers this took place, but it did come to an abrupt end.

One summer while I was visiting him, something happened. It was late and his parents had gone to bed. We shared the sofa bed in the living room. We began by playing and wrestling as any young boys would do. At some point what had started out as playing and having fun, was no longer playing and I wasn't having any fun. At first, I wasn't even sure what he was trying to do, but I did know I didn't like it. He was older, bigger, stronger, and there I was being molested by him. I remember being scared and ready to go home. What I didn't do, was ever visit again during the summer. I actually don't remember ever going back. Need I say he never visited me again either. I never mentioned it to my mom. She went to her grave not knowing what had happened to her baby boy.

I now wonder who Glenn really is, who I really am. The codependent behavior has kept me wearing masks, masks that would conceal my genuine self or what is sometimes known as our child within. The real Glenn

Chapter 2 – When Did It Start?

somehow came to feel unworthy and unlikable. I guess there was always a mask that was likable. If that didn't work, there was an inability to say 'no.' I blame the codependent behavior for not having any boundaries. I wanted others to like me no matter what it took.

I was actually 47 years old before I was able to share what had happened to me that night. By then I was a minister, I was married, and living in Texas. I had planned a tent revival for a Thursday, Friday, and Saturday night in the city where we lived. The Bible commissions us to 'Go ye therefore into all the world.' I just wanted to go out into the community. Erecting a tent and getting some folding chairs allowed us to come from behind the four walls of our brick and mortar church and share the Gospel with some that might not otherwise come to church. In a tent revival, we do a lot of what we would do in a church building, except now we're out in the open. Each night there was a male and female speaker. A dear friend and I were to close out on that Saturday night. In the weeks leading up to the tent revival, I kept having a recurring thought. My life seems to have always been about making a difference and helping others, and this tent revival was to do the same thing. I was troubled because I felt God was telling me if I really wanted to help people, I couldn't have secrets. I knew the very first time I heard those words what they meant. It meant that after all this time, I was going to have to share what had happened that night on the sofa bed. I had to talk about being violated as a young boy. I had to talk about something I thought I would never talk about in public or in the open. I thought it

Chapter 2 – When Did It Start?

was something I would take to my grave. The night for me to preach had come. I was still not sure that I would have the strength to do what I felt like I was being asked to do by God.

Well, there I was, and I had learned that obedience was better than sacrifice. My text that night came for John the 3rd chapter and the 16th verse: "For God so loved the world that He gave His only begotten Son, that whosoever believes in Him should not perish but have everlasting life." The entire verse was not my focus for the evening or the sermon. My main focus was one word in the text. It was the word, "whosoever." I went on to give the subject of my sermon in the form of a question. It was: "Even Me?" There was God's word saying in John 3:16 to me and all who heard it, that God so loved the world (and everybody in it) that He gave His only begotten Son, so that (here it comes) WHOSOEVER, hold it right there. I've already talked about that night when I was a child. At 47 years old there were a lot of things I had done that I wasn't exactly proud of. So while God was expressing the ultimate expression of love to whosoever would believe in Him, I paused to ask, "Even me?" My wife had never heard me mention anything at all about this; I can't imagine what she was feeling having heard it right along with everyone else. I remember apologizing in front of everyone and trying to briefly explain that I wasn't just trying to hide it from her, it was supposed to be hidden from the world. This story was to go to my grave with me. I wasn't even sure until I got up, if I would even have the courage. My desire to be free and liberated was stronger than my fear of sharing the story.

Chapter 2 – When Did It Start?

Of course, I was praying it would help someone. I was lead to do one other thing that night. I'm not sure how many people were there under that tent that night. Just before I concluded, I came down off the platform from which I had delivered my sermon. I went to every individual that was there that night, took him or her by the hand and said, "EVEN YOU!" When those words were said to everyone under the tent, I ran; I'm sure to everyone's dismay. There was a house halfway down the block that was supposed to be a place where drugs were sold. Remember, this was a tent revival, so I was sure they had heard me and everything that was going on. There was a group of people hanging outside and drug dealers or not, they deserved to know "Even them." So I took each of their hands and said, "Even you." That's what liberated me from the dark secret of being molested as a child by a relative. I pray this book will help in the process of liberating me from codependent behavior.

I believe my personal self-image took a blow from that incident. I'm not going to be able to give clinical reasons for what I've gone through, actions I took, and why I did some things in life or make a lot of the decisions that I made. I'm not an expert on codependency, so I can't talk like one. I'm just a man, who, from childhood, didn't realize my self-worth and allowed my codependent behavior to adversely affect my life. I'm not an expert at all, just a person trying to finally let go of the pain.

Let me pause to say something to parents. Please, please, please tell your children that you love them. Love on

Chapter 2 – When Did It Start?

them with all the hugs and kisses you can give them. Tell them how special they are. Affirm how special they are. It probably wasn't common in my generation, and before that, parents would believe that if you had a roof over your head and clothes on your back then that means I love you. I say this with all due respect to a mother that I worshipped the ground she walked on.

Had I gotten those things, would I have spent my young and adult life trying to find love everywhere else? Was love really supposed to cost that much? Why was I willing to pay so much? There were times it cost everything. I'm not sure there's enough of anything to make someone love you and there doesn't seem to be any substitutions for love. I just mean that only love is love. Gratitude isn't love. Showing support and being there isn't love, nor is security love. Remember, you're not reading the words of an expert. I'm just the guy who appeared to have no limits or boundaries when it came to the pursuit of love. It may have helped had I just been able to say no.

The earliest instance seemed innocent, but looking back I'm not sure. There was a girl I liked in middle school when boys were giving bubble gums rings, but not me. I had found a gold ring in the house and my mom let me keep. Well, it seemed like the perfect way to let this girl know I liked her. More importantly, I wanted her to like me. I smile thinking about it because evidently she took the ring home and showed it to her mother. Well, her mom told her to give it back because I may have stolen it. Not long ago, I asked her if she remembered it. I wrestle even now with how a life

Chapter 2 – When Did It Start?

could be so void or deficient of love to do the things I've done. I do see how people can be judged just because someone saw a picture of them in a moment of time. That was the first instance I can think of in which I was trying to get someone to love me.

I'm hearing that voice again telling me that if I want help or I want to be a help that I still can't keep secrets. The reason they are secrets is the embarrassment, shame, sometimes humiliation, and even pain that I feel. I later found out one of the main characteristics of codependency was control. Someone even thought I had the Napoleon Syndrome. I even denied being controlling, and not because I was lying, but because I just didn't see myself as being controlling until I really thought about it. You see, if I fell in love with someone, it pretty much didn't matter if they loved me in the beginning because the process begins to make them love me, and that was at all cost. This is where having some boundaries would have come in handy. I think had I just loved Glenn, had I felt the way about me that I should have felt, I would have been okay. I'm glad that reliving these experiences are also helping me release them and helping me remove that mask that I've hidden behind for years. When you talk about wearing a mask it's often thought of as deception. Well, not all of the time. My masks were worn for protection. Behind the mask was a hurting child. People liked Pastor Keller, they liked the leader of the prayer line, they liked the business owner and the board member, but I didn't think they would like Glenn, and if they didn't he would have been devastated, so he was kept hidden, not to deceive, but to protect.

Chapter 2 – When Did It Start?

Even growing up and going to high school, I remember I had been told that no one in my family was that dark, so approaching girls with any level of confidence, if at all, was out of the question. It didn't help at all when I would hear what was a very popular saying among African Americans when I was young was, "Say it loud, I'm black and I'm proud." It also wasn't unusual to hear some others say, "Let me get out of this sun before I turn black." I heard people trying not to be what I was, and that was dark-skinned. The guys that seemed to be popular and liked, even if it was just in my mind, were what was called light-skinned or brown-skinned, had wavy or curly hair, and could be dumb as a box of rocks, but that was what the girls seemed to like. Sorry brothers, but yes, I was hating back then. Something good probably came out of it. I felt like since no young lady was ever going to look at me and say, "I want him," I learned how to treat a lady. I made having manners and showing the utmost respect and being complimentary a priority, which are traits I carry with me today.

I can't say that there was anyone in particular to be blamed for in the situation, I just described light-skinned and dark-skinned since it was also a sign of the times. I say that because my mom used to save old newspaper clippings. There used to be an African-American newspaper in New Orleans where I grew up, and I found a drawer where mom had saved old newspapers that dated back to when I was a small boy. While reading through the paper I would look at the old classified ads and they would read something like this: *Wanted, light-skinned colored girl for counter help.* Others would

Chapter 2 – When Did It Start?

read: *Light-skinned porter wanted to clean cars on showroom floor.* I think it made some African Americans conclude that being light-skinned was better. If that truly was a mentality, it started long before when I was a little boy. Why did I add that? Put together what I heard as a child, and add to it as a young man feeling like dark skin was not the preference of society or some individuals who just happened not to be dark. Let me fast forward and I will back up, but as far as I'm concerned "Dark skin is in, baby!"

Right now, I'm having to deal with not being able to share every incident or every relationship that clearly pointed out how much I was trying to be loved and how far I would go to feel that love. The ones I highlight may help me make my point and I'm sure also make you shake your head. I'm convinced people don't realize how much pain can be behind the biggest smile. There are times as I write this that I'm going to have to stop and dry my eyes from just remembering that I felt the need to make someone love me, and how I could not have loved myself.

I remember a friend introducing me to a friend that was in town visiting her, and in what was a short period of time I was in love. When it came time for her to go home, I felt we loved each other. She had some things going on at home and she was even considerate enough to ask if I thought she should go back. I told her most assuredly that she should go back because if she didn't, she would always wonder if she should have gone back, and that wouldn't help either of us. I made up my mind that she was coming back. I believe I had the first part of that old saying down pat,

Chapter 2 – When Did It Start?

which said: "If you love something, set it free, and if it comes back, it was yours…." That was the only part I needed to know because she was coming back. Here I go now. The problem as I saw it was that she had young children at the time. Well, at the time I had three part-time jobs; I was a fill-in radio announcer, a cashier at a gas station, and a janitor. My question to myself was, how was I going to take care of her and the children when she came back? We were going to need a place to stay, and of course, everyone was going to need insurance. Where was I going to find a job that would provide all of that? After giving it not much thought, (did you get that?) *not much thought*, I decided to go back into the military. Yes, I had already done my time in the military when I first graduated from high school. Here I was about to reenlist. This time it was not to serve my country, no indeed, it was for love. I would love to tell everyone she came back, we got married, and lived happily ever after, but that's not how it happened. I was so sure. Why would someone go as far as to sign up for military service? If you picked up this book, I hope you did so with the intention that it would be real. If you've never seen it before, you may see how badly someone could need help without anyone even knowing or being able to tell.

One of my marriages was to someone that I had dated after I had served in the military. She felt like I wasn't doing enough even though I was doing my best, so the relationship ended. Well, a year or so had passed and I stopped by for a visit. *'Just a visit,'* I thought. I found myself driving around 200 miles round trip to get to work every day

Chapter 2 – When Did It Start?

after that visit. I got off work and came in the house to "Don't you love me?" and "Don't you want to marry me?" and there I stood like a deer in the headlights only being able to say, "Of course." It couldn't have been more than two or three days later when I found myself standing in front of a preacher in the middle of the week, saying I do. I'm not sure how long it lasted. I wanted it to last. After all, it was what I always wanted, which was to be loved and appreciated. The search was over for everything I needed and had longed for. I was broken and at the time, I didn't know I was broken. Ideally, two healthy people should enter into a relationship. If the two are willing to work hard enough, maybe you can get by with one person being broken. Occasionally, two broken people with hard work and the help of the almighty God can make it. Normally, can you make one whole out of two broken pieces? I've seen people being judged because it looks like they can't stand to be alone. They are criticized for always having to have a man or always having to have a woman that they can't be alone for a minute. Some have been judged harshly for that. I'm sure they're not willing or able to admit the places being lonely and unloved will take you. It will take you to feeling like you wish somebody loved you to wondering what it would take to get someone to show their heartfelt love and appreciation; that would make all the difference in the world.

There was a time that I got love and gratitude confused. Let me be the first to tell you that love is the only thing that is love. I say that before I demonstrate that gratitude is not love. The more I write the harder this is

Chapter 2 – When Did It Start?

getting. I'm talking about the time I married someone a short time after she got out of jail. After all, she was a good person, she came from a good family, and had just made some mistakes. The unconventional reasoning was all she needed was to know someone loved and care for her, someone to give her a fresh start. And what would she be? That's right, she would be eternally grateful. She was walking out of jail into her own place with someone that was going to be there for her and in her corner. She walked into a new place. We even started attending the church where her father had been an associate minister before passing away. It was the church where I was licensed and ordained. It looked like it was working just as planned. I think it was six months later that I came home and she was nowhere to be found. I looked and searched for a week before she finally showed up at home. Not our home, it was her mother's home. She told me where she had been and went on to let me know that church stuff was my life, not her life. It was a rude awakening to find out something I should have already known, and that was gratitude was not love. If you do someone a favor, they express gratitude. I guess in a roundabout way I did her a favor. I ran into a store she was working at some years later. She was a manager, in fact, it was then that she expressed her gratitude. She apologized and thanked me, for she felt if I had not married her and exposed her to a different life, she would have been destined to return to her former life.

    I was over a third of the way through this book when I came back to add this part. I didn't tell this at first because I thought it was too much. It was too hurtful, painful,

Chapter 2 – When Did It Start?

embarrassing, and I was too ashamed to share it. I asked myself, was I just trying to sell a few books, or was I trying to be truly liberated? This is about taking off all of the masks and being totally liberated. I told you I married her a few days after she had gotten out of jail. The rest seems like something you would see on television. I said nothing of my working at the place she was incarcerated and had been for almost four years. It was a job I loved and thought I would retire doing it. The part that would not make it good enough for television was that there was never any physical contact or secret meetings. When it was almost time for her to be released, I actually resigned, almost without giving it a second thought. I knew it wouldn't take long for it to get out that we were together and I would have lost my job anyway. I really wanted to leave out this part because on top of everything else, once I was no longer working there, I went back on visitation day in front of all my former coworkers and those who I felt respected me to visit her while she was still incarcerated. I subjected myself to being searched in front of all the people that, until now, had respected me. If I could compare my behavior to anything, although I have no personal experience, I can only say it had to be like being addicted to crack cocaine. I obviously had no control over what I was willing to do to find love.

There is something about codependent behavior that once you enter someone's life, it is as if you no longer have a life, or that nothing in your life is as important as what is going on in the other person's life. What they needed was more important than what my own needs may have been.

Chapter 2 – When Did It Start?

Something else that didn't work was playing the knight in shining armor. My stories get harder and harder, including the shame and embarrassment, but if I don't take the bandage off it will never heal.

A friend of mine and his wife introduced me to their friend. All she needed was a knight in shining armor. She hadn't lived or grown up in the best place. She had recently gotten a cast taken off of her arm from where her boyfriend had broken it. She needed someone to save her and that's what I was there for. If I were to just rescue her, in return I would get the love I had been searching for. How could I have been totally unaffected? My decisions bring tears to my eyes now. I was so caught up so as to meet someone on Thursday and be married by Monday. There was one family member in particular that didn't like it and would call her when I wasn't there to let her know she would send her a bus ticket to get home. One day, I called the family while she was right there under their nose to express she had her arm broken and suffered other abuses. Now, she was married and in her own home, and everybody was worried. As if it weren't bad enough that codependent behavior had found me married, the worst thing that happened was a child being born into this. Every child deserves to have two loving parents that will work together to give them the upbringing they will need to lead happy and fulfilled lives. What in the hell was I doing, not only to my life, but the lives of those that were being caught in that web? Is there any wonder my life has been troubled? Was there enough of something in me that would keep me from getting other people caught up?

Chapter 2 – When Did It Start?

What's worse than to need help and not get it? I think it's worse that I didn't even realize I needed help. I think it was worse having two eyes and yet, not seeing that something was wrong here. Most, if not all, of that occurred while I was in a backsliding state. I was no longer walking with God. I was no longer preaching and I bet someone is saying, "That was your problem right there." Since when did being saved exempt anyone from problems, or what we more commonly refer to as trials and tribulations? Seeking God helps, but has it stopped anyone completely from making bad decisions? I was saved, preaching, had established a ministry, started a prayer line, fed and clothed countless people, all while needing help and knowing there was a hurting child within me. I wonder if anyone knows there is no hurt like church hurt. I could never subject my child within to that and had to protect him at all cost. I probably could have said something had I known it would have been followed by acceptance and if it had been followed by love. The thought of the pain wouldn't allow me to do it.

So, I just kept wearing the mask that was ever varying and ever concealing. Please don't think I wasn't sincere about everything I did for God or man. I just had to do them behind a mask I felt people would like or even love; a mask that would garner appreciation from those I came in contact with. I wasn't trying to fool anyone, I was trying to just be liked. Finally, I had gotten my life back in line with God's Word. I even returned to preaching.

There was one thing I now regret not doing. There were lots of times based on prayer requests made that I could

Chapter 2 – When Did It Start?

have recommended that person see a healthcare professional, be it physical or mental. Instead, my message was always by His stripes we're healed, and before you think I doubt that, I don't. I just believe healing doesn't take place when I lay my hands on someone. Someone is probably saying, "Of course, not your hands." I just believe God heals when He wants to heal. Every blind eye wasn't open, and every lame person didn't walk. God allowed there to be doctors and even specialists for everything that hurts you and everywhere it hurts. My issues were mental and I needed to be liberated from my thoughts and actions, and whom the Son sets free is free indeed. There are those who are freed and liberated by the wisdom and knowledge God gives, and He gave some special individuals called doctors to maintain the bodies that He created. The stigma associated with mental health was that if you went to see a mental health professional you had to be crazy. Our brains can only handle so many stresses and when there is too much going on, we should actively and aggressively seek people who were put here to help us work through it. Those special individuals who work as mental health professionals have helped a lot of people not get to where the only solution was an overdose of pills. The Lord still works in mysterious ways, like maybe making sure there is a doctor somewhere close by that can help with your needs, and God, therefore, remains the supplier of all your needs through hospitals, doctors, nurses, and clinics.

This time I knew I had it right when I met her. The name I gave her even indicated she was it. There was no

Chapter 2 – When Did It Start?

more rushing to the altar. It took three or four years of hanging out before it was called dating, then another three years or so before getting married. It wasn't even seen as codependent behavior this time. This time, it was love, plain and simple. Saturday mornings I would get up, put a bucket and rag in my car, and drive across town to wash her car and leave a rose on the windshield while she slept. There were the poems I would write. One Valentine's Day I dropped off so much stuff at her job that when I got off the elevator the receptionist wanted the names of all the women that the balloons, candy, flowers, stuffed animals, and card were for. I said, "It's all for the same person," and blew their minds. It was her. The one I wanted to love me more than anyone. I was seeing the same behavior and still wasn't recognizing it just like I hadn't in the past.

One of the things that stands out the most was when hurricane Katrina was headed toward New Orleans. I made sure my mother was safely out of town. She told me she would be going to another state to stay with a relative until it was safe to come back. I faxed an application to a place near there. I had an interview that Saturday morning and if I got the job, I was going to have to figure out where I was going to stay. I arrived at the place where the interview was going to be conducted at about 8:30 and the interview was for 9:00. At 8:45 I got a call from her that she wasn't going to stay there, that she was heading to another state. I missed the interview because by 9:00, I was faxing applications to that state. All of this should have been sounding a lot like days gone by. The second day I was there, I had a job and I was

Chapter 2 – When Did It Start?

given an apartment with six months free rent. It was the following year before the wedding took place. There was no rushing this time. The engagement ring was still on layaway in New Orleans. I had to secretly have it transferred to a store in the new state so that I could pick it up in order to officially propose.

The years began to pass and there were issues that had not been addressed, and they were my issues. Up until now, they were not seen as issues. At a glance, I just looked like a really nice, really charming, loving and giving man. One of the things that would seem to happen is that I would feel as if I wasn't getting back what I was giving. When I really think about it, how was I ever going to get back what I was giving? If I had been keeping score, I always gave away too much. How was I ever going to get that back from anywhere or from anyone? Someone may think that if you put two people with codependent behavior together, they would be the perfect match. You would be wrong. You might be wrong. Or not. Can two broken individuals have a complete relationship? I defer to the professionals and believe anything is possible if you work hard enough.

There I was, married and still starving to be liked, to be appreciated. Something I've tried hard not to do is lay blame anywhere, except for squarely where it belonged, and that was on me. I learned from some of my recent reading on codependency that there was a cycle. You start out as an enabler, then you become a persecutor, and end up a victim. The desire to be liked had gotten the best of me. She went through my phone one night and discovered conversations

Chapter 2 – When Did It Start?

that had taken place that, at times, went right up to the line and may have, on occasion, crossed it. She felt exactly how I would have felt had I found the same things in her phone.

There was an instance where I had bought a couple of gifts. I had begun feeding off of the attention of my friends. To a large number of my friends, Pastor Keller was this and that and liked and admired and appreciated. One of the gifts was for a friend that was job hunting and didn't have a phone for people to call her back and I sent a prepaid phone. The other gift was delivered where one of my friends lived. I was good about posting on Facebook, places I would make deliveries and which city or state I was in. On this particular day, when I posted where I was, I just happened to be near this friend. Once she saw the post, she offered to drive the couple of minutes it would take for her to get there. This is how the second gift came to be. Although she never asked for a thing, when she picked out what she was going to buy, I paid for it. After all, she had just done something nice for me. There I was, the guy who had everyone's phone number and wherever there was a need, I would put on my red cape and boots and fly off to the rescue. It was never about sex. It was about trying to fill a void that had been empty since I was a child.

I have a MoneyGram account where I could send money from my phone. As the pastor of Making A Difference Ministries, I would get the calls when the rent couldn't be paid, lights were about to be turned off, someone didn't have gas money, didn't have milk for the baby, and so on and so on. I've had that account for about three years or

Chapter 2 – When Did It Start?

so. During one of the last MoneyGrams I sent, I decided to go back and add up just how much help I had provided. When I totaled it up, it was just under $5,000.00. That was easy enough to reconcile in my mind that I was a pastor and a Man of God after all. I was always taught that it was in giving that you receive. That's why I was blessed: because of my giving. When in actuality, if my wife couldn't know about it, then I shouldn't have been doing it. When I left, I told her I was tired and unhappy, she eventually told me that she hoped that I would find happiness. I'm sure she thought the happiness I was talking about was in another woman. I can't say it wasn't the same thought that had crossed my mind. It wasn't very long before I realized that the happiness I needed to find was within myself.

We are divorced now, but we communicate on a regular basis, and I've tried to explain codependent behavior. She says I've long since been forgiven, but she doesn't get it. She's not alone; I think very few people get it, even though it's closely related to alcoholism and drug abuse because it started out from the codependent children of alcoholics and drug abusers. The meetings for codependency have the same 12 step program. The difference is no one could see what I was going through. It wasn't alcohol, so you were never going to see me falling over drunk. I've never used drugs so you were never going to see me high or about to overdose. Maybe the people who were on the receiving end of my behavior, the people I would do anything that I possibly could for, saw nothing wrong there. What could possibly be wrong? Yet, I never felt taken advantage of.

Chapter 2 – When Did It Start?

No one begged me. In most cases, they didn't even have to ask.

There were those that would say I needed to do things for myself. The only problem was that I didn't leave anything for myself. For the past few months I've been trying to fix my truck and make much-needed repairs because even though the truck was the way I generated income, it got neglected along with me. I remember I would come home with CD's for my wife to listen to because I really wanted her to get me, to understand me, and it was hard for me because at the first sign that someone was not getting it, the child in me would shut completely down. He was not going to be exposed nor would he be hurt by someone that didn't get it. I heard a story of a man that was a traveling salesman and he was lonely and thought about getting a pet to keep him company, but it couldn't be a dog or a cat because he would be gone too long. He finally decided on some expensive tropical fish. He bought the tank, heater, feeder, and everything he needed to sustain the fish while he was gone. He came home late one night and really didn't feel like going to his bedroom so he got a blanket and curled up on the sofa next to the fish tank. While he slept the heater on the tank malfunctioned. When he awoke the next morning, he found the fish had been boiled to death, and were bloated and floating on top of the water. As he stood there devastated, he asked himself an almost childlike question: "I wonder if the fish cried out during the night and I didn't hear them?" He was right there on the sofa next to them, but he wasn't in the tank and couldn't feel what they felt or

Chapter 2 – When Did It Start?

experience what they were experiencing. I, like the fish, had been crying out.

I remember waking up one Saturday, wrote this poem, and posted it on Facebook:

The Day I Got Tired

When everyone else's life gets all of the attention

Spending what seems like all your time advancing other's positions

You work and you toil to get them to a higher height

Doing all that you can so that they may get it right

Then you wake up one day asking what about me

What about the things I want to do and places I want to see

My codependent self has spread me out far and wide

Instead of being on mine, I was on everybody else's side

That was yesterday and today is brand new

I'll get ahead just doing for me all I tried to do for you

You are not a single person at this point there have been a lot

For my personal survival the madness has to stop

If it appears I'm acting strange it's just me trying to do me

It's just that at some point that's how it had to be.

Chapter 2 – When Did It Start?

When I looked back at it, and I don't know if you hear it, but I sound like someone that may have been stuck in a hole and was desperately trying to get out. I can almost see me sitting at the bottom of a hole screaming at the top of my lungs, "Hello, can anyone hear me? Is anyone out there?" There was a realization of where I was and I was scratching and clawing trying to get out. The pressure must have continued to build because it wasn't long before another poem became a way to cry out again:

Trying Desperately to Cope

I keep poking my head out trying to find a safe place to play

Trying desperately to be attentive to things others do and say

It starts to look okay to venture out, but not too far

I didn't learn my lesson last time and I still bear the scar

Maybe it's safer to stay inside, it's safer to stay hidden

It seems to be the only way most times of protecting My Child Within.

Chapter 2 – When Did It Start?

There were a couple of people who got it. One of them God called home, and may she rest in peace. We met at her job when I was having a procedure done. I stopped by a few days later and dropped a card thanking her for all she had done while I was there and left my number. She called and we became close friends. She had to travel to her sister's 50th wedding anniversary and asked if I would house sit for a couple of weeks and I agreed. When she walked back in the door a couple of weeks later and put everything down, she started looking for the bills she knew had come in while she was away. She found it hard to believe they had all been paid. She knew there was one that could not have been paid: the mortgage. She was wrong, I paid that one, too. We became closer and after a while, we were engaged. I paid the bills that came while she was gone, but from that point on we did everything together.

Well, I did find a way to mess it up. How in the world did I screw that up? Not everyone will consider this messing up, but in hindsight, I do. When we met I had given up on church, but I hadn't given up on God and I don't believe he had given up on me. Almost overnight, I was ready to go back to church and start preaching again. It was as if I dropped it in her lap like a ton of bricks. She had a saying: "I'm not that kind of girl." Well, when I went back to preaching I also became the pastor of a small church. That would mean she would have to become a First Lady. Because I did it both suddenly and abruptly, what I got was, "I'm not that kind of girl." I could have done it better, I could have done it differently, but I didn't and I lost her. I didn't realize

Chapter 2 – When Did It Start?

at the time her relationship with God didn't have to be the same as my relationship was with God. Maybe that's why it's called having a personal relationship with Him, because whatever it is, it is between you and God. Our personal relationships are personal; they are between us and the other person and nobody else's business. I now feel that's exactly how a personal relationship should be: between God and a person and nobody else's business. I only have to prove my love for God to God. I didn't realize that then and I lost her.

I hear from her daughter who lets me know how she and my grandson are doing. She didn't know that the first time she contacted me and mentioned my grandson, I cried just knowing that was how she felt with everything that had happened. It was special that she remembered me in such a way to consider her only child my grandchild. She lives in the house that her mother and I used to share and she's invited me to come over a couple of times, but I don't think I can take that. The thought I can't take most of all is that God called her mom home before I could fix things. Although I have seen and talked to her daughter, brother, sister-in-law, and her nieces, all of whom call me Uncle Glenn; to this day it has been so hard to face them. I haven't seen her parents since she passed away and I want to so bad. Her dad used to call me son. I couldn't find a way to tell them how sorry I was. I thought if God had just given her more time, then maybe I would have realized the mistake I had made and fixed it. I'm just sorry what happened ever happened in the first place. They all loved her and so did I. If any of you ever read this, please forgive me.

Chapter 2 – When Did It Start?

The other person that got it was earlier in my life. She actually told me that she saw it. This was before direct deposit and my entire check was going to her home. My first check actually went there before I did. Our little family consisted of her, her teenage son and daughter, my teenage son, and me. However, back then they were our children, not hers and mine. If you're wondering if I screwed up the answer is yes. We're friends to this day. I remember talking to her about 20 years after we broke up and told her I had a stupid question. When she asked what it was, I said every week my checks came to the house and I never asked where they were or what she did with them. She told me I didn't have to. She said, "You came, all the bills were paid, there were always groceries, the house was clean, the children had everything they needed, and as a matter of fact, their friends thought we were rich. If you came home and needed money, it was there, and if I needed anything I had it." She said our checks took care of everything, that it was so much of a help having me there, and there was no way she was messing that up. Guess she had no reason to think I didn't need any help messing it up; that I have proven capable of doing that all by myself.

There were a few other people that I read another poem to. I played it off as if it was just a nice poem. It was a poem by Charles C. Finn called "Please Hear What I'm Not Saying," and it was actually me crying out. The poem was about the masks we wear that conceal our true and genuine self. About the pain of possible rejection if people really knew that inside was a trembling child and not some strong man.

Chapter 2 – When Did It Start?

It was about keeping that child hidden because you don't want anyone to know. You wouldn't mind others knowing if you knew you would be loved and accepted, but it would be too much pain to take the chance of revealing your child within and not be accepted. So you just continue through life never taking off the mask, never trusting anyone enough to know about that trembling child within.

There were times I felt as if I was crying out at the top of my lungs. Why couldn't I have been direct? Why couldn't I have said what was going on with me? I guess I just never got the feeling that it would be followed by acceptance or love. I was protecting my child within at all cost.

Knowing His Divine Will

Countless times this was the route that

I would drive

It would only be a few hours before at moms

home I would arrive

By now mom would have called if only

to see

To find out how far I had made it and find out how

much longer it would be

Chapter 2 – When Did It Start?

When mom was able she would have prepared my favorite meal

To mom, all of my visits were treated as if they were a big deal

It's still hard following this route knowing that mom is no longer there

No longer sitting in her living room in her favorite chair

Seeing my sister and her children is what takes me to Baton Rouge now

Knowing that we are family we are going to make It somehow

Carol and I both have an emptiness that no one else can fill

So we just thank God for mom and accept His divine will.

Chapter 2 – When Did It Start?

Chapter 3 – How Did I Find Out?

Chapter 3

How Did I Find Out?

Chapter 3 – How Did I Find Out?

I could see how other people would think everything was all right. I actually thought everything was all right. I worked at One Shell Square, a very prestigious investment firm. At the time, it was located in the tallest building in New Orleans and our offices were on the first floor. I came in to work every day wearing my suit, tie, and carrying my briefcase. I was the only African American, I was well respected, and I loved my job. My office was within walking distance of Charity Hospital. It was the place where I think most people in New Orleans were born. I would walk there on a lot of my lunch breaks and visit with those I knew had been admitted to the hospital and pray with them.

I also didn't work very far from Canal Street. It was downtown New Orleans and I believe it was the place where people went shopping before someone came up with shopping malls. Well, it also seemed to be a good place for street preaching. At times, I would go there at lunch or after work and preach on the streets. Across the street from a store called Kraus there was a neutral ground where I would station myself and preach to people as they passed by. That was still only part of what I was involved in. Once a week I did a live broadcast from the local gospel radio station. This was my routine and I carried it out faithfully.

That was until one day, I was on my way to the radio station. I must have been about halfway there when I turned my car around and went back home. My energy felt completely depleted. Had I gone to the radio station I felt like I wouldn't actually work. It's not like there was hard labor to be performed. I would go on air and just minister

Chapter 3 – How Did I Find Out?

for 15 minutes. That's all, just 15 minutes, and I didn't even have the strength. What strength I had left only allowed me to get up every morning, get dressed and go to work. There were no more hospital visits nor was there any more street preaching. How awful was it that I even avoided my Christian friends? I somehow felt like they would tell me that we should pray. Well, I didn't feel like praying. Was it possible that I had gotten so burnt out that I didn't even feel like praying? For as long as I had been preaching, if prayer had been all it took, then I would have been fine. I was tired. I don't know who has ever been tired, and not just tired, but tired for real. Well, I was tired for real. I knew God was my very present help in a time of need. What I also learned was that God had others that could be a help in our times of need. That's why I have so much respect for those in the medical and mental health fields. If you've never seen rock bottom, it's not a pretty sight. I'm really not sure how much lower I could have sunk.

With what must have been my last ounce of strength, I called an EAP line. Employers had what was called the Employee Assistance Program. It was a number you could call and they didn't have to report anything back to your employer. Not feeling like I could go any further and feeling like I was at the end of my rope, I called. The lady on the other end of the phone asked me what I had been going through and she said I appeared to be depressed. She asked me to tell her some of the things I did for pleasure. This may sound familiar to those of you reading this book. I went on to tell her about visiting the hospital, street preaching, and

Chapter 3 – How Did I Find Out?

going to the radio station. Her questions got harder. She asked me what I did for myself, for my own personal pleasure. In other words, she wanted to know, what did I do for Glenn?

There was a really long pause. It seemed like it took me forever to answer. The truth is, I didn't have an answer. I couldn't tell her one single solitary thing that I did for Glenn or my pleasure. I can't tell you how hard that hit me. I might as well have taken a punch from a heavyweight fighter. What I can tell you is why it hit me that hard. My mind immediately went to the fact that although I had a really nice job, worked for a really nice firm in a really nice building, there was something that was wrong. Every morning I got up, put on my suit, and left home looking very professional, but at the time, I only owned one pair of dress socks. I would rinse them out every night and put them back on every morning. With all the concern I had for those at the hospital, those who would pass as I preached on the street, and those who listened to me on the radio, I seemed to have zero concern for me.

I finally gave her an answer that hurt and it hurt a lot. I had to admit that there was nothing I did for myself. Nothing at all. From what I had told her she felt like I had been dealing with something called Codependency. I had never heard of it, but my life had definitely been affected by it. She recommended I start attending Codependent Anonymous meetings and find a therapist. At this point, I was willing to do almost anything to get better. With my one pair of socks on, I was off to my first Codependent

Chapter 3 – How Did I Find Out?

Anonymous meeting. The meetings are the same as those they have for alcohol and drug addictions. Since my eyes had been opened, there was a range of emotions I had been feeling. I felt stupid, silly, and ashamed, to mention a few. I also felt that no one else in the world could possibly be as silly or as stupid.

During the first meeting, I just sat there and cried and cried, and then cried some more. As the people who had been attending regularly got up to speak, they would say "Hello," state their name, and then say, "I'm codependent." I didn't tell you why I was crying. I started crying then for the same reason I'm sitting here, now, in front of my laptop crying. I really wasn't alone. I really wasn't the only one. As the different people went around the circle telling their story, it didn't take long to realize they were telling my story. I felt like I was no longer in a room full of strangers. I was there with people that felt my pain and knew what I was going through. I felt I was in a safe place to tell my story. No one there had a reason to laugh at me or to look at me funny and for sure I didn't feel like I would be criticized. I felt safe enough that, although I had no intention whatsoever of telling a bunch of strangers my business, I did.

I actually said the words: "Hello, my name is Glenn, and I'm Codependent." And everyone responded, "Welcome, Glenn," and I felt like I was part of something special. I mistakenly thought I had sat there and cried all the tears that I could possibly cry, but I was wrong because as I began to share my real story for the first time, the tears started all over again. I thought that being a minister, Man

Chapter 3 – How Did I Find Out?

of God, preacher, and servant of God, had helped me mask my codependency. After all, I was "called" to serve and I was just doing God's will. I started attending meetings regularly and was feeling better. I also found a therapist who, I was able to spend some time with. There were a couple of things she said that stuck with me. Keep in mind, this was a long time ago, but she told me that I didn't have a grey area, that there was no in between for me; things were either black or white, right or wrong.

The next thing she said I will never forget. She told me I could walk into a room with 100 women in it. All of them would be available, 99 of them would be independent, self-sufficient women, and I would leave with the needy one every time. It made me say 'wow.' I think I even said it backwards, wow. I remember a time realizing that I was unable to control the decisions and choices I was making. I thought it would take meeting someone that loved me so much that they wouldn't allow me to try to do it all on my own and bring some balance to my life. I know someday I'm going to be free of this. I don't think I will be able to handle anybody that needs me, from the standpoint of not being able to make it without me.

After all I've been through, it's kind of fuzzy of what a good relationship is, exactly. In my mind, I like to view it as a partnership; two people bringing to the table whatever it is they have to offer and using those resources jointly, whatever they may be, to achieve a common goal. There would be no 'mines' and 'yours' or 'what you do' and 'what

Chapter 3 – How Did I Find Out?

they do.' Instead, it would be 'ours' and 'what we do.' Is that a fairy tale or am I dreaming?

At some point, I stopped going to meetings. I think when I left that job I no longer had the insurance to cover the therapist. When I thought about my Christian upbringing and what I knew about the Word of God, it seemed to be a conflict affirming and constantly reaffirming that I was a codependent and getting the impression that I always would be. I got the 12 step program and I am not saying anything against it, nor will I ever. The Bible says "So a man thinks, so is he." I felt I needed to stop saying I was a codependent. It was only later in life while talking to my friend Mike Rodriguez who shared a story about all the things we are born with as babies. We are born with 10 fingers and toes. We're born with two eyes, two ears, and a mouth, among other things. Then he asked, "Where is that pouch you had when you were born?" I said, "What pouch?" He replied, "The pouch with the codependency in it." I told him that there was no pouch with codependency, because we aren't born with that. I realized then that it was something we picked up later in life. Rather than say I'm codependent, I chose to say I have dealt with codependent behavior. I really should have stayed in the group sessions and should have found a way to continue to see a health care professional.

From then to now, it has not been easy. I think I have an explanation for how I've been able to survive. Many times over the years, I've been told how much I love my truck, having been an over-the-road truck driver, and now owner, for over 25 years. The reality is the truck has been a safe place

Chapter 3 – How Did I Find Out?

for my child within. No matter what was going on, once I made it to the truck everything was all right.

We used to play a game when we were kids called "it." The person that was "it" had to touch someone else by chasing them in order for that person to become "it." The only thing that would prevent that person from being "it" was if they made it to the base. Base could be the stairs, stop sign, or light pole, but if you made it to base, you were safe. Just like with the game "it," whatever may have been going on when I made it to the truck (or base), he (or the child within), was safe from any hurt, harm, or danger.

The truck wasn't the only safe place. There was a place that was the safest place in the whole wide world. On August 29th, 2015, God called my mom home to be with Him, and at that moment, I lost what was the safest place in the whole wide world. Whatever she said or didn't say, did or didn't do, that may have caused me pain or embarrassment when I was growing up, I realized that I was a momma's boy and I wore it like a badge of honor. When mom was able and knew I was coming, all she wanted to know was what I wanted to eat and she would have it all ready for me, plus some. I would lie there on the sofa without a care in the world. Having these safe places kept the pressure from building to the point of being unbearable. I would only be home or any other place for a matter of days, then I'd return to the peace and tranquility of my truck. A nine-to-five would probably make me feel like I was trapped with no hope of escape and would have made me seek help sooner, which is probably how I found out for a second time

Chapter 3 – How Did I Find Out?

that what I really needed was the professional help of a therapist or psychiatrist. All that hurt, pain, and failed attempts, was as if I hadn't learned a thing. I was actually going to try another relationship. I was going to try a relationship without getting any of the help that I really needed, and I was going to continue the facade as if all was sunny and unruffled.

Something happened that I couldn't believe and was almost debilitating. It didn't seem like a really big thing, but it was enough to push me over the top. I got two messages that totally blindsided me; it was one message that said two things. Instead of saying what the first message was, I will say how it made me feel. The message made me feel like I wasn't doing my part. I felt like I was falling short of my responsibility. How could that be? I tried to explain that I didn't know how to do anything else, but my all. When you get me, you get everything. By everything, I mean it included everything: what I should have been using to take care of and handle my own business. It really wasn't uncommon for me to feel like I hadn't done my best, after I felt like I had done my best. What was different this time? Maybe it was in the way it was conveyed. Maybe it was because of a second message.

The second message had been about what I had been doing to help out my ex-wife. It wasn't anything my ex-wife had asked for, but I realized she was going to need financial help and I didn't want her having to go to her family. After all, she gave me 9 ½ years of her life, so as far as I was concerned, she had earned and was entitled to what she was

Chapter 3 – How Did I Find Out?

getting. I wonder what kind of man it would make me, to say I divorced someone and I wasn't doing anything for her, if she needed it or not. We've talked and she appreciated the help, while also looking forward to the day she can tell me that she is all right. I just couldn't see someone that I had spent so much of my life with having to go and ask for money from her family, and God forbid, be made to believe she was having to beg. Whatever that makes me, I don't care because I'm going to keep helping her financially until she is all right.

For the second time in my life, I was backed into a corner and forced to accept my codependent behavior. Did I actually think something was going to change? Is not the definition of insanity doing the same thing over and over thinking there would be a different result? How did I feel? I felt a lot like the alcoholic that just has to have another drink. I felt like a drug addict that just had to have another hit. They know what it's doing to them, after all, they had been told and reminded by everyone, yet their destructive behavior continues. My behavior had proven time and time again to be unsustainable. I couldn't even continue to write checks on my bank account without ever making a deposit. I was constantly giving, giving, giving, with little to no regard for my own needs. Like I said, I was unsustainable.

You've seen us before. You may have even been one of us. Giving, giving, giving, thinking that will make it work. I kept recklessly going on and on. I pray these words will motivate someone to nip it in the bud, to slow the train down before it runs off of the tracks. I will continue to encourage

Chapter 3 – How Did I Find Out?

those feeling like they need help to seek a professional. It was a lot to carry around and a lot to deal with.

There seems to be a running joke throughout my family for a long time. As soon as I get out of the car, walk into the house, or show up at a function, it wouldn't be long before it happened. Someone would blurt out, "How many times have you been married?" I don't know why I called it a joke because it was never funny. I would initially just try to avoid answering as if I didn't hear the question. If it turned out they really didn't know, or someone new was present that didn't really know, I would just lie. Have you ever asked yourself, *"How many people have you hurt?"* without even realizing you have hurt or are hurting them? Is any consideration given to the person you are saying it to, or that you're saying it about? This pain is real and I'm glad to be releasing it.

Leading up to Mother's Day a friend asked how I was doing now that my mom had passed away. I responded, "I will be alright." I got the classic church response: "You are already alright." Well, I wasn't alright because I hadn't, as of yet, done anything significant in order to be alright. A couple of days after mom was laid to rest I was back on the road. I can't even say for sure that I've taken the time that I should have to grieve. I for sure hadn't done anything to get help with my codependent behavior. Could it have been as simple as me just learning to say no? Could there at least have been a balance between the times I said yes and the times I said no?

Chapter 3 – How Did I Find Out?

Never underestimate the challenges associated with dealing with a mental issue. At times saying yes and following through was no problem at all. There were times that I said yes and then had to figure out how I was going to do what I had just said yes to. If you've never experienced what I'm talking about, there is agony at the thought of saying "no" to anyone. If I said no, would they still like me? Even worse, if I said no, would they still love me? If I said no, would I still be seen as the person I had presented myself as? What about the times I said yes and didn't know how I was going to follow though? I should be serving time in jail right now. No, not really. However, if it were possible, I would be serving time for robbing Peter and my only defense would have been to pay Paul, especially when it was money because that money had to come from somewhere.

So which one of my bills was I not going to pay? Which repair was I going to let slide for my truck? Some of you would probably vote to have me committed knowing that I rode around without getting the air conditioner on my truck fixed for over a year. No, I am not going quietly with the men in the white suits to the room with the padded walls. It was only a couple of months ago I fixed a mirror that cost less than $100 that had been broken for months. Oil changes went a little longer than they were supposed to. How was it possible that everything and everyone else was more important than I was?

Chapter 3 – How Did I Find Out?

Mom I'm Going to be All Right

I like talking to mom in the still of the night

I like to let her know her favorite son is going to be all right

I know I'm her only son and it doesn't matter

I know that you know, too, so stop the chatter.

It's been seven months to the day since mom said good bye

It still only takes the thought of her to bring a tear to my eye.

I wonder if she knew I considered her home a safe place to be

A place to deal with all that may have troubled me

Not sure how I came to write the way I do

I'll give mom the credit and you just trust it to be true

Mom worked too hard for me not to be great

So what am I waiting for because once I close my eyes it will definitely be too late.

Chapter 3 – How Did I Find Out?

Chapter 4

Moving Towards Peace

Chapter 4 – Moving Towards Peace

While I'm working to build up the trust and confidence that I should have in myself, I'm learning to depend on God. There's no doubt in my mind that I can trust the God that created me and His word. Unlike anything else in the world, I was created in God's image. I was born with 10 toes, 10 fingers, two eyes, two ears, and a mouth. What I wasn't born with was the codependent behavior that I speak of in this book. Codependency was one of the things, like so many others, that we develop and pick up on our own. My confidence in the God that created me comes from thinking about how special I must have been.

The Bible describes God as having spoken this world into existence. Yet, when it comes to me, it says He formed me out of the dust of the ground and breathed the breath of life into me. When I look in the mirror, I choose to see someone that was fearfully and wonderfully made. I've been loved since before I was born, even if at times I didn't see it. God loved me so much He gave His Only Son. I lost track of my own self-worth, yet I'm able to reestablish my worth when I look to God's Word. How powerful is it to learn in His Word that I'm the head and not the tail, above and not beneath, the lender and not the borrower? I spent far too much time thinking of myself far below where I should have. I did things and made decisions that were not consistent with who God said I was. If I'm going to live the life that I was intended to live, then it's important that I believe in myself.

In his book, "Think and Grow Rich: A Black Choice," Dennis Kimbro tells the story of a little boy sitting in class painting a picture. When the teacher asked what he

Chapter 4 – Moving Towards Peace

was doing, the young boy replied, "Painting a picture of God." The teacher told the young boy that no one knows what God looks like. The young boy replied, "They will in a minute." We've got to believe in ourselves, even when no one else will.

Believing in ourselves obviously can be a challenge sometimes. It was a challenge for me and I finally had to remind myself who I was and whose I was. God never intended for me to live a defeated life. A common saying among some is "I'm waiting on The Lord." I've always been more of the opinion that God has been waiting on me. What would God be waiting on me for? He would be waiting for me to use the gifts and talents that he placed inside me, including all of the things He gave me that would help me be all that I was created to be. I don't want to be like the man He gave one talent to that did not use it, and ended up getting it taken away from him.

I embark on my journey towards peace, a peace that comes with knowing my self-worth. My self-worth will no longer depend on any outside input. I did a lot of people-pleasing and it just about wore me out. I would do this or that, and hope that I would be liked or appreciated. Maybe if I bought something with money that I didn't really have to spend, then they would like me for sure. Self-worth comes along with self-love. It's been really weird because there are people who I know sincerely love me and who I'm admired by. Yet somehow, in my own mind, I wasn't able to love myself.

Chapter 4 – Moving Towards Peace

The Bible says "Be ye transformed by the renewing of your mind." Therefore, I am going through a mind renewal. I'm excited about enjoying the peace God intended for me to have. I'm no longer going to hide behind the mask that concealed the true and genuine Glenn. The relief is coming while I'm writing. I'm being liberated while I'm writing. There is going to be a peace associated with being able to set boundaries for myself, and at the same time learning how to say no without feeling guilty. I wish I could explain the anxiety I experience at the possibility of having to tell someone no. I wondered where I was going to get the money, or whatever else it was that someone needed because when I told them "yes" I had no idea where I was going to get it from.

There are some of you that are going to just shake your heads in disbelief and others who will know exactly what I'm talking about. Right now, I can smell the peace that I'm talking about and I sense that it's near and I can almost taste it and I can't wait to live it. It's a peace that comes with being able to destroy the self-built prison walls that I would hide behind. I'm actually being liberated from the codependent behavior that has kept me bound for all of these years. If you've read to this point, you know it had me in a chokehold and was squeezing the life out of me. I pray I can get someone to understand that whom the Son sets free is free indeed. When I say The Son, of course I mean The Son of God. Not only The Son Himself, but also every one of the resources that He has made available to us. God has blessed me with one of the best psychiatrists known to man

Chapter 4 – Moving Towards Peace

to help guide me through this process and to find answers I so desperately need. It happened to be someone that was right under my nose. For someone who's saying, "I thought you were talking about God giving you peace and liberating you." I most definitely am talking about God doing it. I didn't just come to the reality that God uses people to get His work done on this earth; when you read your Bible you recognize that there are times when He uses some of the most unlikely people. There were people God used in the Bible that would have never made it through the first interview if we were on the selection committee. Would any of those disciples have made the cut?

I need to get really serious here about the day I hit my rock bottom; the day I could no longer deal with the behavior that had caused me so much pain for so many years, the day I arrived at a place that must be the hardest place in the world to get to, and some people never get there. What place am I talking about? The place where I realized I needed help. There is a reason I emphasize how hard it must have been. You would think that I would have gotten there sooner. There were the awful decisions, failed marriages, and October 2016 will mark almost two years that I've lived in my truck, with the exception of a few months. It's where I lived when my wife and I separated. Although both of the previous couple of years I grossed over $190,000.00, my truck was in such a state of disrepair that I'm still trying to get it fixed up.

I'm not sure what you would call it, but for me, it was rock bottom. I wonder if that's where the real journey begins

Chapter 4 – Moving Towards Peace

in most instances. Anyway, there I was, finally realizing I needed help, and another feeling came over me. It was a feeling of regret and disappointment. Here I was, the pastor of Making A Difference Ministries, and the organizer of a live prayer line that has been in existence for at least six years and still operates seven days a week 6:00am every morning to this date. I had been responsible for clothing the needy and feeding the hungry. I had been told by some, I was an anointed Man of God and that whenever I prayed you could feel the anointing. All of that, and I was at rock bottom. I had been there for a little while too, and I needed help then or I wasn't sure I was going to make it much longer.

Back to why I felt regret and disappointment. I have been in the ministry for over 20 years. Not consecutively, but it's time to be real. I needed help, and I mean the kind of help that had me seeing a psychiatrist twice a month and looking for a group to participate in. I thought about all the people that got in prayer lines that I stood at the head of. They would walk up, I'd take their hands, and asked what they wanted prayer for. I may sound like I'm about to doubt God, but nothing could be further from the truth. I'm sure there were people in those lines that possibly needed help as much as I did, if not more. Yes, they were in the right place, and yes, I'm honored I had the opportunity to pray with them. I wonder how many like myself needed help beyond the altar call. I would lay hands on someone, and then tell them to praise God because it (whatever they desired prayer for) was already done. I was believing by faith it was already done.

Chapter 4 – Moving Towards Peace

There is just one thing: I don't know when God decides to heal or work a situation out. I do know God is a healer and He's also God of all. I just admitted to needing help. I prayed and ended up with the best doctor I could have. I've been watching the news and there was a story where someone was refusing medical help for themselves or a child when the treatment or procedure would have saved their lives. It's a choice that people are sometimes faced with, and it's their choice to make. One day there was someone that testified on the prayer line that God told them to stop taking their medication. I told them I could never question whether God told them that or not. However, I did ask that it not be shared on the prayer line as a testimony. I didn't want anyone thinking it was something I was teaching. I felt the doctor should be consulted before discontinuing the use of any prescribed medication. I know this maybe a very delicate subject and I'm trying to treat it as such.

I heard a story once about a city that was expected to flood. The mayor put out an evacuation order. They came to the home of an elderly gentleman who they told to evacuate. His response was that he had prayed to the Lord and that God would save him. In an effort to evacuate as many people as possible, there was no time to stay there and argue with him. By the time the water had gotten into the house, the rescuers came back and asked the elderly gentleman to get into the boat. Once again, he replied that he had prayed to the Lord and that God would save him. Once again, he refused to leave and the rescuers had others to save. When they returned the man was on top of his roof, and although

Chapter 4 – Moving Towards Peace

the boat had returned, he would not get in it, stating again that he had prayed to the Lord and God would save him. Once again, there were others to be saved and the rescuers had to leave. By now the man was standing on the highest point on his roof and only his head was visible. The rescuers showed up in a helicopter and asked the old man to get in. This time spitting out water and blowing bubbles, the old man repeated himself that he had prayed to the Lord and God would save him. He drowned. Upon arriving at the gates of heaven, the old man saw the Lord and couldn't wait to ask the Lord why He let him drown. With a kind of confused look on his face, The Lord responded, "I sent two boats and a helicopter."

I would never question anyone's faith, I can only imagine it was God that gave us doctors, nurses, mental health professionals, and others the knowledge to do what they do. Everything may not have to be signs and wonders. It may just be getting an appointment or a prescription, or like me, spending a couple of hours a month talking to someone who is a psychiatrist. As my ministry moves forward, I will never hesitate to pray with someone that requests prayer. However, I will not hesitate to find out if there is something else we can do. I've wondered about the position that I may have put someone in when I've told them that God has already done it and that they are already alright. Then, when whatever was hurting them still hurt, I'd say, "That's just the symptoms, you're healed." I've never had anyone tell me "You prayed for me last week and it didn't work." That might be like doubting God and questioning

Chapter 4 – Moving Towards Peace

me, or questioning God and doubting me.

    All I'm saying is that there are times people need help and that the medical community can provide that help whether to relieve pain, talk through some issues, or save a life. I believe God uses them just as he uses us as His hands here on earth. Where I am now has taught me a lot and I don't ever want to see anyone suffering unnecessarily when they can be helped. There were things that God allowed me to do even in my broken state while having faults and making bad decisions. God knew I wouldn't be perfect, but he knew I would be obedient. I believe that in what God wants me to do next, I can't be broken; in the next dimension of my life, I will need to be whole with a story of having been broken.

    I'm going to be who God says I am. God never once said I was a Codependent. What He did say was that I was an heir and joint heir with Jesus Christ. There are going to be mountains in our lives, but are we not told that if we have the faith of a grain of a mustard seed that you can say to the mountain, "Be ye removed"? Whatever it was that had me thinking I was codependent and displaying codependent behavior, is a state I do not have to remain in. I know that I can be transformed by the renewing of my mind. I will find out what a healthy relationship is. I will be working out of my truck and not living out of my truck. I will have the things in life that I want and that God desires for me to have.

    There is a time and a season for everything under the sun. I will soon be 56 years old. I've been dealing with

Chapter 4 – Moving Towards Peace

codependent behavior as far back as I can remember. Some would go as far as to think when you've gone through something that long, you will go through it for the rest of your life. I've gone as far as I intend to go on this train. This is my stop and I'm getting off. The decisions I made that you read about were not all of them. There were other bad decisions that should have crushed, ruined, and left me penniless. God will leave you with just enough. He left a little boy with a lunch that comprised of two fish and five barley loaves of bread so that He could feed a multitude of five thousand, not to mention the 12 baskets that were leftover. What about the widow that had a handful of meal left, and said she and her son would eat that and die? Out of obedience, she prepared the man of God a cake and her meal barrel never ran empty. It didn't run over, but it never ran empty.

I've got more than Joseph had when his brothers threw him in a pit. He later rose up to be second in command. Had all God left me with were my health and strength, He would have left me with enough to start over. God considers our past, present, and future when He calls us. I can assure you He called me because I would be obedient, and not because I was perfect. The gifts and callings of God are without repentance. I haven't done anything to make God revoke my being called to the ministry.

Chapter 4 – Moving Towards Peace

Thinking of You

Mom, there is not a day that goes by that I don't think of you.

Even at 55, I'm still learning that every word you said was true.

You were my mom and my best friend in this whole wide world.

You will always hold the title of my #1 girl.

It's been 10 months today since the two of us had to part.

That may not be entirely true since you remain in my heart.

Life without you has not been easy I must admit.

Being your son means I must never quit.

Wherever life takes me, I'm saving you a seat on the front row.

I am the proud son of Sallie Mae Keller and I want the world to recognize and know.

Chapter 4 – Moving Towards Peace

Chapter 5

The Way Out

Chapter 5 – The Way Out

Even in the midst of my dysfunction, my codependent behavior, and my bad decisions, I can see where God has always had an exit strategy designed especially for me. God's Word says He will not put more on us than we can bear for He will make a way of escape. God knew in His infinite wisdom that I would be moving past all of this one day. As sad as it may seem, it was only a couple of years ago I remember telling my best friend that I was unhappy and that I felt like I was just going to be unhappy for the rest of my life. Am I ever glad that I was wrong. I can remember years ago I would listen to Zig Ziglar on cassettes tapes. That's right, it has been a while. I had gotten a couple of his books, but during that time I had more time to read. I would listen to the tapes and read when I could because even then I wanted to be a better person, do better, and have more. It was only later on that I found out it was a requirement that you had to BE before you could DO, and you had to DO before you could HAVE. Never could I have imagined in a billion years that I would someday actually become a Ziglar certified speaker and trainer.

I believe God has had stuff going on in the background of my life for a long time. The stuff God had going on was not really for then, but that it was all for now. It was for after I had gone through what I had to go through. It was for after I learned some things about myself and about life. It was as if God was getting me ready for something. God didn't allow me to go through everything that I have gone through to kill me. It was more to mold me, shape me, and make me into a vessel that He could use for His divine

Chapter 5 – The Way Out

purpose and plan. I remember something growing up in church that after you have been tried by the fire, you shall come forth as pure gold.

Well, there I was, on a day much like most of my days at the time. I was depressed and feeling hopeless. I happened to look at my twitter feed and saw where the Ziglar Corporation was looking to train people as Ziglar Legacy Speakers and Trainers. I still haven't figured out how I could feel so hopeless and depressed, yet wanted to become a motivational speaker. It can take a while sometimes to learn you can't circumvent the plan and purpose God has for your life. The tweet invited people to a webcast hosted by Tom Ziglar. Somehow, I already knew it was something that I wanted. I guess I just wanted to know what most people wanted to know. What does it cost? As God's plans go, I happened to have the investment required to become certified.

To go a little further, I hadn't long come into possession of it, and there were some other things I could have done with the money. In talking with my best friend, she pointed out sometimes God gives us a seed to sew into ourselves. That's exactly what I did. I got in touch with the people at the Ziglar Corporation and more or less said sign me up. Did I mention at this time I was depressed and feeling hopeless? I thought about when God asked Abraham to sacrifice his son Isaac. God didn't even tell Abraham where he was going. God just told Abraham to go to a place that He would show him. Please believe me when I tell you that I didn't know where I was going. I have to admit to not really

Chapter 5 – The Way Out

knowing what I was doing. I sure didn't know I was going to a place that God would show me.

The certification took place over a four-day period, lasting from Monday until Thursday. Up until then, I had been a truck driver. I drive what is more commonly referred to as an 18-wheeler. I actually had to go buy a couple of pairs of pants and a few shirts just to have something to wear. When I initially walked in, I could not have felt more out of place. The people I found myself in class with were people who had already been successful speakers, authors, business owners, and there I was, a truck driver. It didn't take very long to find out I was in a room with some of the most amazing people on the planet. The son and daughters of Mr. Ziglar: Tom, Cindy, and Julie, I can claim as my siblings. We hadn't even made it to lunch break before all these amazing people had me feeling I belonged and deserved to be there as much as anyone.

There were some things that I was going to need, and this is where God allowed me to obtain the knowledge I was going to need for where He was going to take me. During those four days, I found out I was part of an entirely new family. By the end of the week, I no longer felt depressed and hopeless. It was as if I had become a new man. Now I wanted to walk, talk, and act like a new man. One of my first changes was that I no longer wanted to weigh 326 pounds. Over the next three months, I lost 26 pounds. Shortly after that, Tom and I had a conversation about juicing, and I decided to try it. I lost an additional 70 pounds. In a short span of time, I lost my mom and went through a divorce. In

Chapter 5 – The Way Out

my hour of need, I turned to food and gained a big chunk of weight back. I'm so glad that one of the things that I learned was that failure was an event and not a person. With that being said, the weight was going to come back off. I have learned that there is a time and season for everything. I do believe that God has given me a gift to speak; however, I believe I also feel like it wasn't the time to fully use that gift. I was certain when I got my certification I would be speaking all over the place. Instead, I'm finding out now that it was all part of God's exit strategy for my life. David was chosen to be king as a young boy, but he wasn't ready to be king. I was being given tools that I would use later in life to glorify God.

The four days of training were just the beginning. There were some things that God and life were going to teach me. It's appearing that in God's plan not only was I going to have to come out whole and healed, but my life's mission was going to be helping as many as I could to be healed and made whole. There is no way I was going to ever understand why I had to experience the pain, shame, and embarrassment that I endured. I couldn't make sense or understand how I could possibly make so many bad decisions. Had I not gone through what I did, I could have mistaken my gift in speaking as just another source of income, when in fact, it was meant to be so much more. Having experienced all that I went through, I believe my gift was meant to be liberating, as well as life changing. I can speak now with a certain conviction and passion that you only get when you have gone through something and come out on the other side with the victory.

Chapter 5 – The Way Out

God told Solomon that he could ask for anything that he wanted. Solomon chose to ask God for wisdom. God told Solomon that because he didn't ask for riches that He would give him that, too. Can I share with you what it was I asked God for a long time ago? God didn't tell me I could ask for anything. I didn't ask for houses or land, I didn't ask for riches, fame or fine automobiles. I simply asked God for a voice. Yes, that was all I wanted, was a voice. I saw things in the world and in my community that I felt like a voice would change. I saw situations that I felt I could play a role in turning around if I just had a voice. If I had a voice, I could speak into the lives of people and begin to see those lives and communities change. I wasn't going to be able to do that with money, but I felt like if I had a voice I would be able to.

It was with a voice that Dr. King said, "I have a dream." It was with a voice that President John F. Kennedy said, "Ask not what your country can do for you, but ask what you can do for your country." It was with a voice that President Barack Obama said, "Yes we can." It was with a voice that my mentor, Mr. Zig Ziglar, said, "You can have everything in life you want if you would just help enough other people get what they want." Who am I to think that my voice could bring about change? Who was Moses when God told him to go tell Pharaoh to "Let My people go?" It is with a voice I hope to see the graduation rate rise and the murder rate go down. I ended up at the doorstep of Ziglar Corporation because my prayer was being answered. I asked for a voice because I wanted to say something. I had to get to a place where I would know what to say.

Chapter 5 – The Way Out

In God's infinite wisdom and exit plan for my life, He provided me with what I was going to need to say. God didn't go to sleep at the wheel of my life to let the devil wreck the car. God was there when I was going into and through my dysfunction, and He had a plan for my coming out. He knew the places I would have to go. He knew that people I would have to meet. I had to feel the pains and frustrations of His people in order to properly address the pains and frustrations of His people. I learned a long time ago that you have to go through some things before you can talk about some things. Now that God has made his exit strategy clear to me, I am able to share it. I now have a renewed level of passion and enthusiasm.

Of all the things in life I could desire and that I could ask for, why a voice? It is with a voice that I'm able to let people everywhere know that we are who we are and where we are because of what goes into our minds. That we can change who we are and where we are by changing what goes into our minds.

I've been involved in ministry for over 20 years. For God so loved the world that He gave His only begotten Son that whosoever believes in Him would not perish, but have everlasting life and will get you to heaven. Having goals will make you successful.

I heard it said that if you don't know where you are going that any road will get you there. There was absolutely no way I would share with you all of my pains and sorrows and not share with you hope for your tomorrows. Had God given me a voice when I asked for it, I'm not sure what I

Chapter 5 – The Way Out

would have done with it. People underestimate what it is to have goals. When I showed up at Ziglar Headquarters, I was at what was probably the lowest point of my life. Although it wasn't a three-day revival, but a four-day training, I left there revived. I left there knowing how to establish a plan for my life. Instead of being a wandering generality, I was able to become a meaningful specific.

You might be surprised to know according to the best research that less than three percent of Americans have written goals and less than one percent rewrite their goals on a daily basis. A goal that is not written down is a wish that doesn't have any power behind it. The lack of clearly defined goals causes the problem of being involved in a lot of activity with very little, if any, productivity. When you understand the formula for setting goals, you can set a goal for anything. We've got to have goals. It means that any long lasting success achieved, any balance in our life, any objective accomplished, happens because we had a goal. Have you ever considered that everyone has a goal? The drug addict's goal is to get another fix; the child's goal is to not get caught doing something bad by their parent. I wonder if you ever heard the story of the processionary caterpillars. They got their name because they follow each other in a procession. An experiment was done where the processionary caterpillars were placed around the base of a flowerpot. Inside the flowerpot, pine needles were placed, which is the favorite food of the processionary caterpillars. They followed each other around the base of the flowerpot for 12 hours, 36 hours, 72 hours, and eventually up to seven days

Chapter 5 – The Way Out

until they all died of exhaustion and starvation with their favorite food only three inches away.

Are we paying attention to who we're following and where they are leading us? One of the major benefits of setting specific goals is the power it releases in our energy, our creativity, our problem-solving skills, and our productivity. I absolutely struggle because I want so badly for people to know how important it is to have goals and how they can change your life. I know because of how they changed my life. I know astronauts didn't get to the moon by just wandering around. Tiger Woods didn't become a champion golfer by simply shooting a few rounds of golf on Sunday. Michael Jordan didn't obtain his level of success on the basketball court by shooting a few hoops every once in a while. Sir Edmond Hillary didn't become the first person to reach the peak of Mt. Everest because he just went for a little hike one day. No, they each had clear goals and worked diligently to get there. We may not dream of achieving national fame, but any amount of success that you pursue takes solid goal setting.

Allow me to run some math past you. Don't think I've lost my mind, but what is 3 x 4? I hope everyone said 12. What if I asked you, what does 133,647 x 5,689 equal? Obviously, if you pull out that calculator on that cell phone or get a paper and pen, you can tell me the answer because you understand the multiplication formula. Oh, by the way, the answer is 760,317,783. My point is goal setting has a formula. Once you understand the formula, then you can set and achieve any of your goals. Setting goals is a seven-step

Chapter 5 – The Way Out

process that I would be glad to share with your employees, church or organization. Learning to set goals became so liberating for me because as I explained in the beginning of this book, so much of my life was consumed by what I did for others. When I learned to set goals, it became personal. The goals I set had to be my own. Setting goals gave me hope and allowed me to see a bright future. Having a voice and not being able to get myself together would probably not have worked. Having goals led me from where I was, to places that I wanted and needed to be.

If we were sitting in an auditorium, I would ask you by show of hands, how many of you can think of something you could be doing in the next two weeks that could make your life better? Now, how many of you can think of something you could do in the next two weeks that could make your life worse? This is important because you would have just told yourself that you have the power to make your life better or worse. Not your boss, not the economy, not your spouse, not your mother or father – YOU. The choice is ours! You can have hope that you can always make a change in you. I made a change in me and you have the power to make that change.

Story time. John Jones arrived at the airport early. Having a few minutes to spare, he walked up to some old-timey scales in front of the magazine store, stepped on them, inserted a coin, and down came a slip of paper with his weight and fortune. The fortune read: "Your name is John Jones, you weigh 188 pounds, and you are going to catch the 2:20 to Boston." He was astounded because of the

Chapter 5 – The Way Out

information being correct. He figured this must be a trick, so he stepped back on the scales, inserted another coin and down came his fortune: "Your name is still John Jones, you still weigh 188 pounds, and you are still going to catch the 2:20 to Boston." Now he was more puzzled than ever. Sensing a trick, he decided to 'fool' whoever or whatever was responsible. He went into the men's room and changed clothes. Once again, he stepped on the scales, inserted his coin, and down came his fortune: "Your name is still John Jones, you still weigh 188 pounds – but you've missed the 2:20 to Boston."

Too many times, we get distracted by life and miss out on all the good things life has to offer us. Let this remind you that you truly can be the best you and have all the good things life has to offer you. There are eight things that come to mind that most people want in life. To be happy, to be healthy, to be prosperous, to be secure, to have friends, peace of mind, good family relationships, and hope for a better tomorrow. There is no elevator to those things. There is no easy way to consistently have all of the good things you want out of life. We must work for them. We must take the stairs and those stairs must be built on a solid foundation of your faith. Did you know the tallest buildings have the deepest foundations? When your life is built on a strong foundation and when, (not if) you hit a rough patch in life, you won't fall down into the basement, you will land on a solid foundation to rebuild your life.

There are absolutely steps you can take to reach the things in life you want. One of them is your self-image. Story

Chapter 5 – The Way Out

time again. There was a balloon salesman in Chicago. Whenever balloon sales would slow down, he would release a balloon to get the attention of the crowd. Well, things slowed down, and the balloon salesman released a red balloon. It got the attention of those standing around and sales picked up. Things slowed down again and the balloon salesman released a yellow balloon, and once again it got the attention of the crowd and sales picked up again. A young African-American kid walked up, got the balloon salesman's attention, and asked if he released a black balloon, would it go up? The balloon salesman got down on one knee so he could look the young man eye to eye. The balloon salesman said to the young African-American kid that it's not what's on the outside of the balloon that makes it go up, but it's what's on the inside.

A victory list is a confidential list you keep of the big and little victories in your life. Writing them down is important. When you have one of "those" days, you can review the list and encourage yourself to persevere. Something called Automobile University has been a great help to me. It's using the time I spend in the truck or in my car to better myself by listening to educational, spiritual, and inspirational podcasts, CD's, and things like that.

God did something that I am eternally grateful for, and that is He put all of us on a level playing field. I've never heard it put better the way Edgar A. Guest expressed it in the poem "Equipment." The poem eloquently explains that if you were to examine the equipment of the greatest of the great, no matter how far you go back in history, you would

Chapter 5 – The Way Out

find that they have two arms, two hands, two legs, and two eyes, just as you and I. It tells me I have the same potential to be as great as anyone that has ever lived.

...Figure it out for yourself, my lad,
You've all that the greatest of men have had,
Two arms, two hands, two legs, two eyes
And a brain to use if you would be wise.
With this equipment they all began,
So start for the top and say, "I can."...

- *Excerpt from Edgar A. Guest "Equipment"*

This book may reach the hands of some that got caught up in my dysfunction. It was not intentional. For a long time I didn't even realize I was broken. I may have hurt, or at the very least, disappointed you, and that was not my intention. For that, I apologize. I'm better now and pray that I have not lost, nor will I ever lose your friendship.

I pray this book becomes a Best-Helper more so than a Best-Seller. Those who may be struggling with codependent behavior as I was, may be at a loss for the bad decisions, the mistakes and the lack of self-worth. Even more importantly, know that there is hope. Know that there is a way out and that you can have victory. If the Son therefore shall make you free, ye shall be free indeed. John 8:36 (KJV)

Chapter 5 – The Way Out

Moving My Mountains

Moving My Mountains

About The Author
GLENN C. KELLER

My name is Glenn C. Keller and I was born in New Orleans, LA., home of The Mardi Gras and affectionately known as The Big Easy. I have one sister Carol Ann Keller and two sons Glenn C. Keller, Jr. and Tadaro L. Keller.

I grew up in The Stronger Hope Baptist Church, which was not an option back then, and I am grateful. I was educated in the public school system and graduated from Warren Easton Fundamental High School.

About 10 days following graduation, I enlisted and served in The United States Army. After serving my country, I came home and served my community as a Criminal Sheriff's Deputy. On April 5, 1986, I was ordained and served The Lord as a minister of The Gospel of Jesus Christ. I went on later with my then wife, Tomlyn Cross Keller, to become the founder of Making A Difference Ministries. The Ministry was about people serving people. Out of that ministry grew a live prayer line which still takes place at 6am every morning.

Fast forward a few years and I was honored to become a Ziglar Certified Speaker and Trainer and I believe that added depth to my ministry by actually giving people a plan of how to set and achieve their goals. My future plans include doing everything I can, by the grace and help of God to continue to make a difference in the lives of God's people.

To Correspond with the Author

Glenn C. Keller
P.O. Box 27
Alvarado, TX 76008

Glenn C. Keller

Ziglar Certified Speaker/Trainer

504.982.2380 PH

800.236.1196 Fax

glennckellerzlc@gmail.com

www.ziglarcertified.com/glennkeller

Moving My Mountains

Moving My Mountains

Moving My Mountains

Disclaimer & Copyright Information

Some of the events, locales and conversations have been recreated from memories. In order to maintain their anonymity, in some instances the names of individuals and places have been changed. As such, some identifying characteristics and details may have changed.

Although the author and publisher have made every effort to ensure that the information in this book was correct at press time, the author and publisher do not assume and hereby disclaim any liability to any party for any loss, damage, or disruption caused by errors or omissions, whether such errors or omissions result from negligence, accident, or any other cause.

Scripture references are copyrighted by www.BibleGateway.com which is operated by the Zondervan Corporation, L.L.C.

All poems and quotes, unless otherwise noted, should be attributed to Glenn C. Keller.

Cover illustration, book design and production
Copyright © 2016 by Tribute Publishing
www.TributePublishing.com

Moving My Mountains

"I can do ALL THINGS through Christ who strengthens me."
Philippians 4:13

Moving My Mountains

www.ingramcontent.com/pod-product-compliance
Lightning Source LLC
Chambersburg PA
CBHW021133300426
44113CB00006B/417